Your Florida Guide to

Bedding Plants

SELECTION, ESTABLISHMENT, AND MAINTENANCE

Robert J. Black and Edward F. Gilman

Florida Cooperative Extension Service
Institute of Food and Agricultural Sciences
University of Florida

University Press of Florida
Gainesville / Tallahassee / Tampa / Boca Raton / Pensacola / Orlando / Miami / Jacksonville

Published in cooperation with the University Press of Florida

Printed in the United States of America on acid-free paper

03 02 01 00 99 98 6 5 4 3 2 1

Library of Congress Cataloging-in-Publication Data
Black, Robert J. (Robert John), 1942–
    Your Florida guide to bedding plants: selection, establishment
    and maintenance / Robert J. Black, Edward F. Gilman.
        p.   cm.
Originally published: Gainesville, Fla.: University of Florida, 1996
Includes bibliographical references (p.) and index.
        ISBN 0-8130-1641-X (pbk.)
        1. Bedding plants—Florida. I. Gilman, Edward F. II. Title.
    SB423.75.U6B53 1998
    635.9'62'09759—dc21   98-25885

Graphic Design: David Dishman
Copy Editor: Robin Sweat

The Florida Cooperative Extension Service at the University of Florida's Institute
of Food and Agricultural Sciences is a partnership of county, state and federal
government which serves the citizens of Florida by providing information and
training on a wide variety of topics. In Florida, the Extension Service is a part of
the University of Florida's Institute of Food and Agriculture Sciences with
selected programs at Florida Agricultural and Mechanical University (FAMU).
Extension touches almost everyone in the state from the homeowner to huge
agribusiness operations in such areas as: food safety, gardening, child and family
development, consumer credit counseling, youth development, energy conservation, sustainable agriculture, competitiveness in world markets, and natural
resource conservation.

The University Press of Florida is the scholarly publishing agency for the
State University System of Florida, comprising Florida A&M University, Florida
Atlantic University, Florida International University, Florida State University,
University of Central Florida, University of Florida, University of North Florida,
University of South Florida, and University of West Florida.

University Press of Florida
15 Northwest 15th Street
Gainesville, FL 32611
http://nersp.nerdc.ufl.edu/~upf

Table of Contents

Introduction

Photo 1: Container-grown plants can add a splash of color to a porch, deck or patio.

Bedding plants, with their seemingly infinite variety of flower color and plant form, fit into almost any landscape. These plants may be grown in containers to add a splash of color to a porch, deck or patio area (**Photo 1**). They can be enjoyed as fresh- and dry-cut flowers and can be a very rewarding hobby.

Bedding plants can be annuals, biennials or perennials. *Annuals* are plants which are grown from seed, produce flowers and seed, and die in one growing season. *Biennials* complete their life span within 2 years, and *perennials* last for 3 years or longer. However, certain plants can be annuals, biennials or perennials depending on the locality or purpose for which they are grown.

Bedding plants are especially versatile in Florida. Many of them bloom during winter months, contributing splendidly to a colorful landscape and producing flowers for home decorations. Others grow and flower during the trying months of June, July, August and September, persistently blooming through the heat and heavy rains of summer.

Photo 2: Plants that love cool temperatures such as petunias should be planted in the fall, winter or early spring.

Cultivation of bedding plants in Florida differs from most states because Florida has three climatic regions. During winter, nights are cool with an occasional freeze in central and south Florida and frequent freezes in north Florida. In early spring and late fall nights are cool, whereas high night temperatures, heavy rains, and high relative humidity are typical during summer and early fall. Careful attention must be given to these climatic conditions if bedding plants are to be grown successfully in Florida. Petunias, pansies and snapdragons that grow well and flower under cool night temperatures (45-65°F) should be planted in the fall, winter and early spring (**Photo 2**). Bedding plants such as gazania, amaranthus, torenia, portulaca, celosia, crossandra, periwinkle and coleus that can tolerate

7

flowering plants such as geraniums and begonias. Although these plants may grow outdoors for more than one year in mild climates, they should be replaced with new, vigorous, disease- and insect-free plants each season. This will eliminate tall, unsightly plants and reduce the buildup of pathogens and insects.

While Florida gardeners are fortunate to have abundant sunshine and mild winters, they must contend with infertile sandy

Photo 4: Plants such as salvia can be planted year-round in central and south Florida.

Photo 3: Plants that love warm temperatures such as celosia should be planted in late spring or early summer.

high temperatures and humidity can be planted in late spring or early summer (**Photo 3**). Some plants such as wax begonias and salvias grow relatively well during both hot and cool seasons and can be planted year-round in central and south Florida (**Photo 4**).

Florida's winter temperatures in the central and southern portions of the state are often not low enough to kill

Above: Masses of colorful bedding plants add brilliance and a welcoming note to the front of a home.

home gardener should allocate more time for maintenance once the decision is made to grow bedding plants. ■

soils, periodic heavy rains and plant pests which necessitate regular scouting and spot treatment. The addition of bedding plants to the landscape will greatly increase maintenance. The

Below: Flower-filled beds and containers create refreshing oases of color around pools and patios.

Where to Use Bedding Plants

Photo 5: Bedding plants create attractive flower beds.

Bedding plants should complement the home and other plants in the landscape. They should not be placed indiscriminately throughout the landscape so that they stand out more than any other feature. This is particularly important in the public area (that area in the front of the house) where all plantings should accent the house, not compete with it for attention. Some landscape designers limit bedding plants in the public area to planter boxes and areas within foundation plantings **(Photo 6)**. Large islands of bedding plants in the front lawn should be avoided because they tend to focus attention away from the house.

Beds of flowering plants add considerable color and interest when planted near porches, patios, terraces and decks. If space around these outdoor living areas is limited, bedding plants can still be enjoyed by growing them in pots, tubs, planter boxes and hanging baskets **(Photo 7)**.

Bedding plants can be very effective when used as borders along fences and shrubs **(Photo 8)**. The background provided by the dark color of a stained

Bedding plants for containers should have short, compact growth habits and long bloom periods. If you choose to mix two or more different kinds of bedding plants in the same container, select those that flower simultaneously and that have similar sun and water requirements.

wood fence or the green foliage of shrubs enhances the color of flowers. Because borders are usually viewed from one side only, they are easy to construct. The lowest growing bedding plants are planted in the front, medium size in the middle, and the tall plants in the back of the bed.

Attractive flower beds can be created with bedding plants (**Photo 5**). Flower beds are usually designed to stand alone and be viewed from several sides. They are more difficult to construct than borders and are best used in formal landscapes.

Other uses of bedding plants are for edging along walks and driveways (**Photo 9**) and for adding a splash of color in or around vegetable gardens. In addition to making vegetable gardens more attractive, they are a good source of cut flowers for indoor arrangements. ■

Photo 6: Limit use of bedding plants in the public area to planter boxes and areas within foundation plantings.

Photo 7: Bedding plants can be enjoyed on decks by growing them in pots, tubs, planter boxes and hanging baskets.

Photo 8: A border of bedding plants can be very effective when planted along a row of shrubs.

Photo 9: Sidewalks and driveways can be edged with bedding plants.

13

Site Selection and Bed Design

Success in growing bedding plants depends on the characteristics of the planting site. The amount of sun or shade, soil moisture and soil type dictate the kinds of bedding plants that can be successfully grown at a particular site. Although bedding plants have different requirements, most will grow and flower best on well-drained sites which have exposure to full sunlight or partial shade. Bedding plants will do very poorly when heavy rains continuously keep the planting beds saturated with water. With the exception of a few shade-tolerant bedding plants, most planted in shady areas will be weak and spindly, with few flowers.

Photo 10: Straight, angular-lined beds can be used when the overall design is straight and angular.

Photo 11: Curved, free-flowing beds are restful to the eye.

presented on pages 56 - 61. Bedding plant choices for both north and south Florida gardens are given. Remember that these are only suggestions and it is a good idea to visit gardens, nurseries and garden stores in your area for ideas on plants to try in your flower garden.

The shape of beds and borders will greatly influence the character of your landscape. Straight, angular lines are usually uninteresting and can be monotonous because they are repeated in walks, drives and property lines. However, when the landscape's overall design is composed of straight lines, angular lines can be used in beds and borders to complement this design scheme (**Photo 10**).

Curved or free-flowing beds and borders are restful to the eye and create a relaxing feeling which contributes to an informal, natural effect (**Photo 11**).

Sketching your flower bed and border designs allows you to make mistakes on paper, not on the landscape site. Sample plans for a border, corner and island bed using either warm season or cool season plants are

Photo 12b: Use the hose to experiment with different shapes for beds or borders.

After you have determined the size and shapes of beds and borders, they can be laid out in the landscape with the help of a garden hose **(Photo 12a)**. Simply outline the shapes of the beds and borders on the ground with a flexible garden hose **(Photo 12b)** and dig and remove grass or other plants inside the outlined area **(Photos 13a - 13d)**. ∎

Photo 13a: Start removing grass or other plants inside the bed by digging along the inside edge of the hose, defining the outside edge of the bed.

Photo 13c: Once the sod has been loosened, it can be removed in pieces and stacked in a wheel–barrow for easy transplanting or composting.

Photo 13b: An efficient method of removing the remaining sod is to make vertical cuts around small sections of turf and then push the shovel horizontally under the sod to loosen it.

Photo 13d: When the bed area has been cleared of all sod, it is ready for additional preparation prior to planting.

Photo 14: Beds should be tilled or spaded several weeks before planting.

Bed Preparation

Beds should be spaded or tilled at least six inches deep several weeks before planting (**Photo 14**). Florida's sandy soils have very low nutrient and water-holding capacities. Incorporation of 2 to 3 inches of organic matter such as compost or peat into planting beds will increase nutrient and water-holding capacities of these soils (**Photo 15**).

Garden soils, especially in recently developed areas, are frequently infertile. Flower beds should be fertilized prior to planting or at planting time and then on a monthly basis (**Photo 16a**). Apply 6-6-6 or a similar complete fertilizer at the rate of 2 pounds per 100 square feet of bed area. Application rates for higher analysis fertilizers are presented in **Figure 1**. Controlled-release fertilizers are ideal for Florida's sandy soils. Plants usually grow much better with a continuous nutrient supply. These fertilizers also help with maintenance, as applications are required less often than with rapid-release fertilizers. Controlled-release fertilizers can be incorporated uniformly throughout the soil before planting and applied on the soil surface of established plantings.

Suggested fertilizer application rates	
Fertilizer Analysis	**lbs/100 sq. ft.**
6-6-6	2.0
8-8-8	1.5
10-10-10	1.2
12-4-12	1.0
12-12-12	1.0
15-30-15	0.8
16-4-8	0.8
16-8-24	0.8
20-20-20	0.6
25-5-20	0.5

Figure 1.

. . . .
Photo 15: Organic matter is incorporated into the bed to increase the nutrient and water-holding capacities of the soil.
. . . .

Spread the organic matter and fertilizer evenly over the bed's surface and spade or till them into the soil to a depth of 6 inches (**Photo 16b**), then level the soil with a garden rake (**Photo 16c**).

Bedding plants can be damaged by nematodes. These microscopic worms are present in most soils in Florida and are likely to reach damaging levels when susceptible plants are grown **repeatedly** in the same area. Treating beds with a soil fumigant is highly desirable prior to planting. However, most fumigants are restricted-use pesticides and must be applied by a professional pesticide applicator.

Other options for controlling nematodes include soil solarization and replacement of nematode-infested soil in beds (Dunn, 1992). Soil solarization is a non-chemical way to reduce soil pest populations, but it takes a lot of

work and the area must be left bare 4 to 8 weeks during the summer. Clear polyethylene is used to cover moist soil that is ready to be planted. The heat generated by sunlight hitting the soil

. . . .
Photo 16a: Beds should be fertilized prior to or at planting time, and then on a monthly basis.
. . . .

will be trapped and the soil temperature will be high enough to kill many nematodes in the upper few inches of the bed. Replacement of nematode-infested soil with sterile soil or potting mix is a simple and fast method of managing nematodes, however, nematodes eventually will reinfest the "clean" soil.

Another approach to reducing nematode damage to bedding plants is to avoid planting nematode-susceptible plants. The susceptibility of some bedding plants to a common species of root-knot nematodes is presented in the **Bedding Plant Selec-** **tion Guide**. This information should be used as a general guide, since it takes into account only one species of root-knot nematodes and different varieties and cultivars of bedding plants vary greatly in their susceptibility to damage by root-knot nematodes (Goff, 1936). ∎

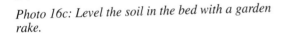

Photo 16c: Level the soil in the bed with a garden rake.

Selection

It is difficult for the average home gardener to germinate seed and grow seedlings; consequently, most gardeners purchase large seedlings or young plants. Before purchasing bedding plants, the home gardener should decide how the plants will be used in the landscape. Bedding plants should serve as an accent to the landscape, not as a dominant feature in the setting. Those used around the home should harmonize with the setting, and colors should blend with each other and with the home.

When selecting bedding plants for beds or borders, it is best to limit the choice to as few kinds as possible. Combinations of many flower colors and plant forms can distract from the overall appearance of the display. Keep in mind that attractive flower beds can be created by using one plant species (**Photo 18**).

The color wheel (**Figure 2**) can be used to obtain pleasing flower color combinations. Primary colors are red, blue and yellow. Orange, green and violet are called secondary colors because they are combinations of two primary colors. For example, yellow and red are combined to produce orange.

Photo 17: Plants grown in 4-inch pots will quickly fill a bed and help prevent weed growth.

Photo 18: Attractive beds can be created by using one plant species.

"Tint" refers to a light value and is accomplished by adding white to the pure color on the color wheel, while "shade" is a dark value and is created by adding black to the pure color on the color wheel. Black, white and grey are neutrals and are compatible with any color. Light colors and tints tend to attract attention, as do bright, vivid colors.

There are three basic color schemes for mixing flower colors. A *monochromatic color scheme* consists of different tints and shades of one color on the color wheel. It includes the entire range of the color and is seldom achieved in its pure form in the landscape. An example of an incomplete monochromatic color scheme would include white and pink flowers with a background of dark pink.

Analogous color schemes combine colors which are adjacent or side-by-side on the color wheel. An analogous color scheme could include red, orange-red, red-orange, orange and yellow-orange. This color scheme could be achieved by using orange-red zinnias or gerbera daisies against a red brick house.

The complementary color scheme combines colors directly across the color wheel. For example, orange and blue would be complementary colors. A complementary color scheme may be achieved by combining orange calendulas with blue pansies.

Colors can be used to visually change distance perspective. Warm colors and light tints like red, orange and yellow advance an object or area toward the observer. These colors and tints placed near the foundation of a house would make the house appear closer to the street. Cool colors and deep shades like blue and green cause objects to appear to recede, and can be used to make the house seem farther away from the street. Cool colors are restful, while warm colors express action and are best used in filtered light or against a green or dark background.

Another characteristic to take into consideration when selecting bedding plants is flower form. Most bedding plant flowers can be classified as either *spike form* or *round form*. Examples of bedding plants with spike form flowers include salvia, snapdragon and plume type celosia. Bedding plants with round form flowers far exceed those with spike flowers and include such favorites as petunias, pansies, marigolds, begonias and impatiens. Bedding plants with spike flowers have very strong vertical lines and should be used sparingly to accent bedding plants with round form flowers.

Flower beds should be prepared before plants are purchased. Allowing plants to remain in their original containers for prolonged periods after purchase can have a negative effect on their performance after planting. Purchase plants when you're ready and plant them as soon as possible, preferably within twenty-four hours.

After beds are prepared and the kinds and quantity of bedding plants to be planted are determined, purchase good quality plants. Look for young, healthy, disease- and insect-free plants with dark green foliage. It is not necessary that plants be in bloom when pur-

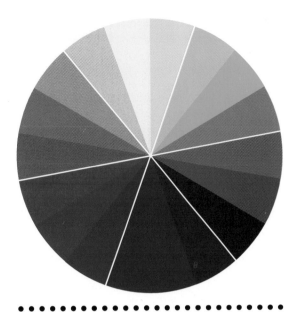

Figure 2. The color wheel is a useful tool for selecting color combinations that work well together.

chased. If plants are reduced in price and have been subjected to water stress or are tall and spindly, they are certainly not a bargain and should not be purchased. Plants with yellowing in between the veins of the leaves may be exhibiting symptoms of nutrient deficiency and should also be avoided. Plants that have been improperly maintained or held too long seldom recover, and if they do they will never reach their full potential. This is true especially with celosias, marigolds, pansies, salvias, snapdragons and zinnias.

Bedding plants can be purchased in compartmentalized plastic flats (cell packs) (**Photo 19**) or in larger containers such as 4-inch pots. The plants grown in 4-inch pots are usually more expensive, but they are larger and therefore will produce more flowers sooner than plants grown in cell packs. As a result, beds established with plants grown in 4-inch pots are attractive sooner and for a longer period of the growing season than beds planted with plants grown in cell packs. An-

Photo 19: Bedding plants can be bought in compartmentalized plastic flats such as these.

other advantage of selecting plants grown in 4-inch pots is that because they are larger than cell pack plants, they will cover the bed sooner and help to control weeds (**Photo 17, page 22**).

Seasonal adaptation should be considered when purchasing bedding plants. Cool-season plants such as snapdragons and pansies that do well during winter are poor selections when purchased in March or April. To help select the correct bedding plant for a particular season, consult the **Bedding Plant Selection Guide, page 30**.

Selection of bedding plants should be greatly influenced by the available light in an area. Some plants, such as marigold and ageratum, perform best in full sun. Others, such as coleus and dahlia, grow best in areas receiving several hours of morning or afternoon sun. There are no flowering plants that will perform well under heavy shade.

However, plants such as crossandra and tuberous begonia grow best in areas receiving no direct sunlight. Optimum and acceptable light levels for many bedding plants are presented in the **Bedding Plant Selection Guide**.

Florida residents living within close proximity to beach-front areas need to select bedding plants that are more tolerant of high winds, salt spray and irrigation water containing high levels of salt. Unfortunately, there is limited information on the tolerance of many bedding plants to these harsh growing conditions. However, a few have proven tolerant when tested on a beach-front area in Florida and the results are presented in **Figure 3.** (Tjia & Rose, 1987). ■

Salt Tolerant Bedding Plants

Blanket Flower (*Gaillardia* spp.)

Dusty Miller (*Senecio cineraria*)

Gazania (*Gazania rigens*)

Geranium (*Pelargonium x hortorum*)

Gerbera (*Gerbera jamesonii*)

Lisianthus (*Eustoma grandiflorum*)

Periwinkle (*Catharanthus roseus*)

Figure 3.

Plants for Special Uses & Conditions

There are bedding plants for most landscape uses and growing conditions. Some are low-growing and suitable for edging walks and driveways; others are tall and excellent for backgrounds. Still others do well when grown in pots and hanging baskets and some even endure the poor growing conditions found indoors. There are bedding plants that tolerate seaside growing conditions, shade or root-knot nematode infested soil. The following selected lists are designed to help you choose the best plants for your purposes and growing conditions. Refer to the **Selection Guide** for additional information.

Bedding Plants for Edging and Low Borders

Ageratum, Flossflower (*Ageratum houstonianum*)

Alyssum, Sweet Alyssum (*Lobularia maritima*)

Begonia, Wax or Fibrous (*Begonia x semperflorens-cultorum*)

Candytuft (*Iberis* spp.)

Celosia (dwarf types)

Dianthus (*Dianthus* spp.)

Dusty Miller (*Senecio cineraria*)

Gazania (*Gazania rigens*)

Globe Amaranth (*Gomphrena globosa*)

Lobelia (*Lobelia erinus*)

Marigold (dwarf types) (*Tagetes* spp.)

Pansy (*Viola x wittrockiana*)

Petunia (*Petunia x hybrida*)

Rose Moss, Portulaca (*Portulaca grandiflora*)

Snapdragon (dwarf types) (*Antirrhinum majus*)

Wishbone Flower, Torenia (*Torenia fournieri*)

Zinnia (Dwarf types) (*Zinnia* spp.)

Bedding Plants for Rock Gardens

African Daisy, Cape Marigold (*Dimorphotheca sinuata*)

Ageratum, Flossflower (*Ageratum houstonianum*)

Begonia, Wax or Fibrous (*Begonia x semperflorens-cultorum*)

Candytuft (*Iberis* spp.)

Dianthus (*Dianthus* spp.)

Lobelia (*Lobelia erinus*)

Pansy (*Viola x wittrockiana*)

Petunia (*Petunia x hybrida*)

Rose Moss, Portulaca (*Portulaca grandiflora*)

Stock (*Matthiola incana*)

Wishbone Flower, Torenia (*Torenia fournieri*)

Verbena (*Verbena x hybrida*)

Bedding Plants for Cut Flowers

Ageratum, Flossflower (*Ageratum houstonianum*)

African Daisy, Cape Marigold (*Dimorphotheca sinuata*)

Baby's Breath, Gysophila (*Gypsophila paniculata*)

Black-Eyed Susan, Gloriosa Daisy (*Rudbeckia hirta*)

Blanket Flower, Gaillardia (*Gaillardia* spp.)

Browallia, Amethyst Flower (*Browallia speciosa*)

Calendula (*Calendula officinalis*)

Calliopsis, Coreopsis (*Coreopsis tinctoria*)

Candytuft (*Iberis* spp.)

Carnation (*Dianthus caryophyllus*)

Celosia (*Celosia* spp.)

Chrysanthemum (*Dendranthema x grandiflora*)

Cosmos (*Cosmos* spp.)

Dahlia (*Dahlia* hybrids)

Delphinium (*Delphinium elatum*)

Dianthus (*Dianthus* spp.)

Gerbera Daisy, Transvaal Daisy (*Gerbera jamesonii*)

Globe Amaranth (*Gomphrena globosa*)

Godetia (*Clarkia* spp.)

Hollyhock (*Alcea rosea*)

Marigold (*Tagetes* spp.)

Pansy (*Viola x wittrockiana*)

Snapdragon (*Antirrhinum majus*)

Spider Flower (*Cleome hasslerana*)

Statice (*Limonium sinuatum*)

Stock (*Matthiola incana*)

Strawflower (*Helichrysum bracteatum*)

Sweet Pea (*Lathyrus odoratus*)

Zinnia (*Zinnia* spp.)

Bedding Plants for Hanging Baskets and Tubs

Alyssum, Sweet Alyssum (*Lobularia maritima*)

Black-Eyed Susan Vine, Thunbergia (*Thunbergia alata*)

Browallia, Amethyst Flower
(*Browallia speciosa*)

Geranium (*Pelargonium x hortorum*)

Impatiens (*Impatiens wallerana*)

Lobelia (*Lobelia erinus*)

Petunia (*Petunia x hybrida*)

Verbena (*Verbena x hybrida*)

Bedding Plants for Fragrance

Alyssum, Sweet Alyssum (*Lobularia maritima*)

Carnation (*Dianthus caryophyllus*)

Heliotrope (*Heliotropium arborescens*)

Nicotiana, Flowering Tobacco
(*Nicotiana alata*)

Petunia (*Petunia x hybrida*)

Stock (*Matthiola incana*)

Sweet Pea (*Lathyrus odoratus*)

Sweet William (*Dianthus barbatus*)

Bedding Plants for Attractive Foliage

Amaranthus, Joseph's Coat
(*Amaranthus tricolor*)

Begonia, Wax or Fibrous (*Begonia semperflorens-cultorum*)

Coleus (*Coleus x hybridus*)

Dusty Miller (*Senecio cineraria*)

Geranium (*Pelargonium x hortorum*)

Ornamental Cabbage and Kale
(*Brassica oleracea*)

Bedding Plants for Indoors

Begonia, Wax or Fibrous (*Begonia semperflorens-cultorum*)

Black-Eyed Susan Vine, Thunbergia
(*Thunbergia alata*)

Browallia, Amethyst Flower
(*Browallia speciosa*)

Coleus (*Coleus x hybridus*)

Impatiens (*Impatiens wallerana*)

Wishbone Flower, Torenia
(*Torenia fournieri*)

Bedding Plants for the Seaside

Blanket Flower, Gaillardia (*Gaillardia* spp.)

Dusty Miller (*Senecio cineraria*)

Gazania (*Gazania rigens*)

Geranium (*Pelargonium x hortorum*)

Gerbera, Transvaal Daisy
(*Gerbera jamesonii*)

Lisianthus (*Eustoma grandiflorum*)

Periwinkle, Vinca (*Catharanthus roseus*)

Bedding Plants for Partial Shade

Begonia, Wax or Fibrous (*Begonia x semperflorens-cultorum*)

Black-Eyed Susan Vine, Thunbergia
(*Thunbergia alata*)

Browallia, Amethyst Flower
(*Browallia speciosa*)

Candytuft (*Iberis* spp.)

Coleus (*Coleus x hybridus*)

Crossandra (*Crossandra infundibuliformis*)

Dahlia (*Dahlia* hybrids)

Foxglove (*Digitalis purpurea*)

Impatiens (*Impatiens wallerana*)

Nicotiana, Flowering Tobacco
(*Nicotiana alata*)

Wishbone Flower, Torenia
(*Torenia fournieri*)

Bedding Plants Resistant to Damage by Root-Knot Nematodes

Ageratum, Flossflower
(*Ageratum houstonianum*)

Black-Eyed Susan, Rudbeckia
(*Rudbeckia hirta*)

Blanket Flower, Gaillardia (*Gaillardia* spp.)

Calliopsis, Coreopsis (*Coreopsis tinctoria*)

Marigold (*Tagetes* spp.)

Bedding Plants for Dried Flower Arrangements

Baby's Breath (*Gypsophila paniculata*)

Cockscomb (*Celosia cristata*)

Globe Amaranth (*Gomphrena globosa*)

Goldenrod (*Solidago* spp.)

Statice (*Limonium sinuatum*)

Strawflower (*Helichrysum bracteatum*)

Sunflower (*Helianthus annuus*)

Bedding Plant Selection Guide

Common name: African Bush-Daisy, Daisy-Bush
Botanical name: *Gamolepis chrysanthemoides*
North Florida planting months: March - May
Central Florida planting months: March - May
South Florida planting months: September - March
Cold tolerance: Tender
Light requirement: Full sun
Soil requirements: Average to very dry soil
Flower color: Yellow
Leaf color: Green
Height: 2 to 4 feet
Plant spacing: 2 to 3 feet
Notes: Requires pruning and pinching to maintain shape. Virtually indestructible plant that thrives in hot, dry areas.

high Salt tolerant

Common name: African Daisy, Cape Marigold
Botanical name: *Dimorphotheca sinuata*
North Florida planting months: March - April
Central Florida planting months: March - April
South Florida planting months: September - March
Cold tolerance: Tender
Light requirement: Full sun
Soil requirements: Light, sandy, well-drained
Flower color: White, yellow, orange, salmon, rose
Leaf color: Dark green
Height: 12 inches
Plant spacing: 12 inches
Notes: Moderately damaged by root-knot nematodes. Withstands drought well, but prefers cool temperatures.

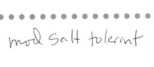

Yellow = North Florida
Orange = Central Florida
Red = South Florida

mod salt tolerant

Common name: Ageratum, Flossflower
Botanical name: *Ageratum houstonianum*
North Florida planting months: April - May
Central Florida planting months: March - April, September - October
South Florida planting months: November - February
Cold tolerance: Tender
Light requirement: Full sun to partial shade
Soil requirements: Well-drained
Flower color: White, blue, pink, lavender
Leaf color: Green
Height: 6 to 18 inches
Plant spacing: 12 to 18 inches
Notes: Not damaged by root-knot nematodes. Not very heat resistant.

Common name: Alyssum, Sweet Alyssum
Botanical name: *Lobularia maritima*
North Florida planting months: February - March
Central Florida planting months: February - March, September - November
South Florida planting months: October - February
Cold tolerance: Hardy
Light requirement: Full sun to partial shade
Soil requirements: Well-drained, performs well in poor soils
Flower color: White, pink, lavender, purple
Leaf color: Bright green
Height: 6 to 12 inches
Plant spacing: 6 to 12 inches
Notes: Very lightly damaged by root-knot nematodes. Excellent for edging beds, borders, walks and drives.

Common name: Amaranthus, Joseph's Coat
Botanical name: *Amaranthus tricolor*
North Florida planting months: April - May
Central Florida planting months: March - April
South Florida planting months: November - February
Cold tolerance: Tender
Light requirement: Full sun
Soil requirements: Well-drained
Flower color: Red
Leaf color: Green, yellow, purple/red, variegated
Height: 1 to 4 feet
Plant spacing: 12 to 18 inches
Notes: Very heavily damaged by root-knot nematodes. Tolerates heat and drought.

Common name: Aster, China
Botanical name: *Callistephus chinensis*
North Florida planting months: March
Central Florida planting months: February
South Florida planting months: October-February
Cold tolerance: Tender
Light requirement: Full sun to partial shade
Soil requirements: Well-drained
Flower color: Blue, lavender, white, pink, yellow, red, blue
Leaf color: Blue-green, green
Height: 1 to 3 feet
Plant spacing: 1½ to 2 feet
Notes: Select cultivars that are resistant to fusarium wilt and viruses.

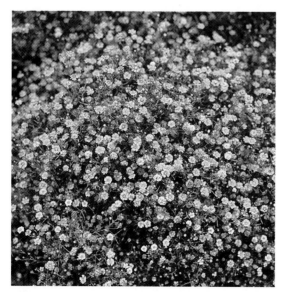

Common name: Baby's Breath, Gysophila
Botanical name: *Gypsophila paniculata*
North Florida planting months: February - March
Central Florida planting months: February - March, November - December
South Florida planting months: August - December
Cold tolerance: Hardy
Light requirement: Full sun
Soil requirements: Moist, alkaline, well-drained
Flower color: White, pink
Leaf color: Green
Height: 1½ to 3 feet
Plant spacing: 3 feet
Notes: Heavily damaged by root-knot nematodes. Excellent cut flowers for arrangements.

Common name: Balsam, Touch-Me-Not
Botanical name: *Impatiens balsamina*
North Florida planting months: April - July
Central Florida planting months: March - August
South Florida planting months: February - September
Cold tolerance: Tender
Light requirement: Full sun to partial shade
Soil requirements: Well-drained, light and sandy
Flower color: Red, white, pink, salmon, purple, lavender
Leaf color: Bright green
Height: 1 to 3 feet
Plant spacing: 1 to 1½ feet
Notes: Very heavily damaged by root-knot nematodes. Flowers are brightly colored and resemble small camellia flowers.

- -

Common name: Begonia, Hybrid Tuberous
Botanical name: *Begonia tuberhybrida*
North Florida planting months: March - May
Central Florida planting months: February - March
South Florida planting months: October - January
Cold tolerance: Tender
Light requirement: Partial shade to full shade
Soil requirements: Well-drained
Flower color: Red, white, pink, salmon, orange, yellow, bicolors
Leaf color: Green
Height: 6 to 18 inches
Plant spacing: 6 to 12 inches
Notes: Excellent for planting in shady beds and borders.

- -

modsalt

Common name: Begonia, Wax or Fibrous Begonia
Botanical name: *Begonia x semperflorens-cultorum*
North Florida planting months: April - August
Central Florida planting months: March - May, September - October
South Florida planting months: October - March
Cold tolerance: Tender
Light requirement: Full sun to partial shade
Soil requirements: Well-drained
Flower color: Red, white, pink, salmon, rose, bicolors, picotee
Leaf color: Green, purple/red, variegated
Height: 6 to 18 inches
Plant spacing: 6 to 12 inches
Notes: Hybrid cultivars can be planted in full sun or partial shade. Standard cultivars perform best in partial shade.

33

Common name: Black-Eyed Susan, Gloriosa Daisy, Coneflower
Botanical name: *Rudbeckia hirta*
North Florida planting months: April - June
Central Florida planting months: March - May
South Florida planting months: February - April, October - November
Cold tolerance: Hardy
Light requirement: Full sun
Soil requirements: Well-drained, tolerates poor and dry soil
Flower color: Yellow, orange, red, rust/bronze
Leaf color: Green
Height: 2 to 3 feet
Plant spacing: 1 to 1½ feet
Notes: Not damaged by root-knot nematodes. Flowers are long-lasting and make excellent cut flowers.

Common name: Black-Eyed Susan Vine, Thunbergia
Botanical name: *Thunbergia alata*
North Florida planting months: March - May
Central Florida planting months: March - May
South Florida planting months: February - April
Cold tolerance: Tender
Light requirement: Full sun or partial shade
Soil requirements: Well-drained, moist, high in organic matter
Flower color: White, yellow, and orange with or without dark purple or black centers
Leaf color: Dark green
Height: 6 to 10 feet
Plant spacing: 1 to 1½ feet
Notes: Very lightly damaged by root-knot nematodes. Tropical vine that climbs by twining stems.

high salt tolerance

Common name: Blanket Flower, Gaillardia
Botanical name: *Gaillardia* spp. and hybrids
North Florida planting months: March - May
Central Florida planting months: February - March
South Florida planting months: February - March
Cold tolerance: Tender
Light requirement: Full sun
Soil requirements: Well-drained, sandy soil
Flower color: Red, orange, yellow
Leaf color: Green
Height: 1 to 2 feet
Plant spacing: 1 to 1½ feet
Notes: Not damaged by root-knot nematodes. Tolerates heat, drought and infertile soil.

high - salt tolerant

Common name: Blue Daze
Botanical name: *Evolvulus glomeratus*
North Florida planting months: April - August
Central Florida planting months: March - September
South Florida planting months: January - December
Cold tolerance: Tender
Light requirement: Full sun to partial shade
Soil requirements: Sandy and well-drained
Flower color: Blue
Leaf color: Blue-green
Height: 6 to 12 inches
Plant spacing: 1½ to 2 feet
Notes: Susceptible to fungus disease during the rainy season. Keep foliage dry. Flowering is slightly reduced in partial shade. Flowers close late in the day.

Common name: Browallia, Amethyst Flower
Botanical name: *Browallia speciosa*
North Florida planting months: April - May
Central Florida planting months: March - April
South Florida planting months: February - March, September - November
Cold tolerance: Tender
Light requirement: Partial shade
Soil requirements: Well-drained
Flower color: White, blue, purple
Leaf color: Green
Height: 1 to 2 feet
Plant spacing: 6 to 12 inches
Notes: Trailing growth habit makes it an excellent plant for hanging baskets.

mod. Salt tolerant

Common name: Calendula, Pot Marigold
Botanical name: *Calendula officinalis*
North Florida planting months: February - April, September - October
Central Florida planting months: February - March, November - December
South Florida planting months: December - February
Cold tolerance: Hardy
Light requirement: Full sun
Soil requirements: Well-drained
Flower color: Orange, yellow, white
Leaf color: Green
Height: 12 to 18 inches
Plant spacing: 6 to 12 inches
Notes: Heavily damaged by root-knot nematodes. Performs well in containers and makes excellent cut flowers.

Common name: Calliopsis, Coreopsis, Tick-seed
Botanical name: *Coreopsis tinctoria*
North Florida planting months: March - May
Central Florida planting months: March - September
South Florida planting months: February - April
Cold tolerance: Hardy
Light requirement: Full sun
Soil requirements: Well-drained; tolerant of poor soil
Flower color: Yellow, red, pink, purple, orange, bicolors
Leaf color: Green
Height: 1 to 3 feet
Plant spacing: 6 to 12 inches
Notes: Not damaged by root-knot nematodes. Taller cultivars may need support. Remove faded blooms to prolong blooming.

Common name: Candytuft
Botanical name: *Iberis* spp.
North Florida planting months: October - February
Central Florida planting months: October - February
South Florida planting months: October - January
Cold tolerance: Hardy
Light requirement: Full sun or partial shade
Soil requirements: Well-drained
Flower color: White, lilac, crimson, pink, carmine, purple and rose
Leaf color: Dark green
Height: 10 to 15 inches
Plant spacing: 6 to 12 inches
Notes: Lightly damaged by root-knot nematodes. Flowering declines during hot weather.

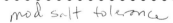

mod salt tolerance

Common name: Carnation
Botanical name: *Dianthus caryophyllus*
North Florida planting months: November - February
Central Florida planting months: November - February
South Florida planting months: October - January
Cold tolerance: Hardy
Light requirement: Full sun
Soil requirements: Fertile, well-drained
Flower color: White, yellow, red, pink, violet, bicolors
Leaf color: Gray green
Height: 2 feet
Plant spacing: 1 to 2 feet
Notes: Lightly damaged by root-knot nematodes. Grow tall cultivars for cutting and dwarf cultivars for beds and borders.

Common name: Chrysanthemum, Garden Chrysanthemum, Florists' Chrysanthemum
Botanical name: *Dendranthema x grandiflora (Chrysanthemum x morifolium)*
North Florida planting months: March - April, September - October
Central Florida planting months: Not recommended
South Florida planting months: Not recommended
Cold tolerance: Tender
Light requirement: Full sun to partial shade
Soil requirements: Well-drained
Flower color: Orange, pink, purple, red, white, yellow
Leaf color: Green
Height: 1 to 2 feet
Plant spacing: 1½ to 2 feet
Notes: Pinch young plants to promote bushiness.

●●●

Common name: Cockscomb, Crested Celosia
Botanical name: *Celosia cristata*
North Florida planting months: April - July
Central Florida planting months: March - November
South Florida planting months: March - November
Cold tolerance: Tender
Light requirement: Full sun
Soil requirements: Well-drained; tolerates poor, dry soil
Flower color: Red, orange, pink, yellow
Leaf color: Green, purple/red
Height: 6 inches to 2 feet
Plant spacing: 6 to 12 inches
Notes: Very heavily damaged by root-knot nematodes. Excellent for cutting and drying for flower arrangements.

●●●

Common name: Cockscomb, Plume Celosia
Botanical name: *Celosia plumosa*
North Florida planting months: April - July
Central Florida planting months: March - November
South Florida planting months: March - November
Cold tolerance: Tender
Light requirement: Full sun
Soil requirements: Well-drained; tolerates poor, dry soil
Flower color: Red, orange, pink, yellow
Leaf color: Green, purple/red
Height: 6 inches to 2 feet
Plant spacing: 6 to 12 inches
Notes: Very heavily damaged by root-knot nematodes. Make long-lasting cut flowers that hold their color well when dried. 'New Look' has red flowers and stems and grows 18 inches tall.

Common name: Coleus
Botanical name: *Coleus x hybridus*
North Florida planting months: April - August
Central Florida planting months: April - August
South Florida planting months: March - September
Cold tolerance: Tender
Light requirement: Partial shade (will tolerate full sun with plenty of irrigation)
Soil requirements: Fertile and well-drained
Flower color: Usually blue (flowers insignificant)
Leaf color: Bronze, red, yellow, green, orange, purple, salmon, brown
Height: 1 to 2 feet
Plant spacing: 1 to 2 feet
Notes: Heavily damaged by root-knot nematodes. Grown for their vibrant, multi-colored leaves. Foliage may fade in full sun.

Common name: Cosmos, Mexican Aster
Botanical name: *Cosmos bipinnatus*
North Florida planting months: April - May
Central Florida planting months: February - March, September - October
South Florida planting months: November - February
Cold tolerance: Tender
Light requirement: Full sun
Soil requirements: Does best in dry, infertile soil.
Flower color: Pink, lavender, white, magenta-red
Leaf color: Green
Height: 1 to 4 feet
Plant spacing: 1 to 1½ feet
Notes: Very lightly damaged by root-knot nematodes. May require staking. Plant among other plants to reduce need for staking.

Common name: Crossandra, Firecracker Flower
Botanical name: *Crossandra infundibuliformis*
North Florida planting months: May - August
Central Florida planting months: April - August
South Florida planting months: March - September
Cold tolerance: Tender
Light requirement: Partial shade to full shade
Soil requirements: Well-drained
Flower color: Yellow, salmon, orange
Leaf color: Green
Height: 1 to 3 feet
Plant spacing: 1 to 1½ feet
Notes: Pinch growing tips to encourage compactness.

Common name: Cupflower, Nierembergia
Botanical name: *Nierembergia hippomancia*
North Florida planting months: April - July
Central Florida planting months: March - July
South Florida planting months: March - August
Cold tolerance: Tender
Light requirement: Full sun to partial shade
Soil requirements: Well-drained with high organic content
Flower color: Blue-violet, purple, white
Leaf color: Green
Height: 6 to 12 inches
Plant spacing: 6 to 12 inches
Notes: Tender perennial that can be grown as an annual. Excellent plant for edging beds and borders. Can also be used as ground cover, in window boxes, and in hanging baskets. Will not flower in winter months.

• •

Common name: Dahlberg Daisy, Golden Fleece
Botanical name: *Dyssodia tenuiloba*
North Florida planting months: April - July
Central Florida planting months: March - July
South Florida planting months: March - August
Cold tolerance: Tender
Light requirement: Full sun
Soil requirements: Well-drained
Flower color: Bright yellow
Leaf color: Emerald green
Height: 4 to 8 inches
Plant spacing: 9 to 12 inches
Notes: Heat and drought tolerant. Excellent low-growing plant for edging beds and borders. Foliage has lemony scent. Good in baskets and planter boxes.

• •

Common name: Dahlia
Botanical name: *Dahlia* hybrids
North Florida planting months: April - May
Central Florida planting months: February - March, October - November
South Florida planting months: September - January
Cold tolerance: Tender
Light requirement: Full sun to partial shade
Soil requirements: Well-drained
Flower color: Red, yellow, white, pink, salmon, lavender, orange, purple
Leaf color: Green
Height: 1 to 6 feet
Plant spacing: 1½ to 2 feet
Notes: Taller cultivars are popular as cut flowers. Dwarf cultivars are commonly grown from seeds as annuals.

Common name: Delphinium
Botanical name: *Delphinium elatum*
North Florida planting months: February - March
Central Florida planting months: February - March
South Florida planting months: December - February
Cold tolerance: Hardy
Light requirement: Full sun
Soil requirements: Moist and fertile
Flower color: White, blue, purple and pink
Leaf color: Bright green
Height: 2½ to 5 feet
Plant spacing: 8 to 15 inches
Notes: Very heavily damaged by root-knot nematodes. Flowers are valued for cutting to make fresh-flower arrangements.

Salt tolerant - good long blooming season

Common name: Dianthus, China Pink, Sweet William
Botanical name: *Dianthus* spp.
North Florida planting months: October - March
Central Florida planting months: November - March
South Florida planting months: November - January
Cold tolerance: Hardy
Light requirement: Full sun to partial shade
Soil requirements: Well-drained
Flower color: White, pink, salmon, purple, red, lavender, bicolors
Leaf color: Green, gray-green
Height: 6 to 18 inches
Plant spacing: 6 to 12 inches
Notes: Lightly damaged by root-knot nematodes. Flowers have fringed petals and are faintly fragrant.

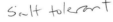

Salt tolerant

Common name: Dusty Miller
Botanical name: *Senecio cineraria*
North Florida planting months: April - May
Central Florida planting months: February - May
South Florida planting months: October - March
Cold tolerance: Tender
Light requirement: Full sun to partial shade
Soil requirements: Well-drained
Flower color: Yellow
Leaf color: Silver/gray
Height: 6 to 12 inches
Plant spacing: 6 to 12 inches
Notes: Performs well in dry soil and tolerates heat. Versatile border plant, good longevity.

Common name: Foxglove
Botanical name: *Digitalis purpurea*
North Florida planting months: February - March
Central Florida planting months: February - March
South Florida planting months: December - February
Cold tolerance: Hardy
Light requirement: Full sun or partial shade
Soil requirements: Moist and fertile
Flower color: Purple, white, pink, yellow, magenta, lavender
Leaf color: Dark green
Height: 2 to 5 feet
Plant spacing: 1 to 1½ feet
Notes: Good background plant for beds and borders.

mod. Salt tolerance   (rabbits like)
to high?   planters only

Common name: Gazania
Botanical name: *Gazania rigens*
North Florida planting months: March - May
Central Florida planting months: February - May, September - October
South Florida planting months: November - May
Cold tolerance: Tender
Light requirement: Full sun
Soil requirements: Well-drained
Flower color: Red, yellow, white, pink, orange, rust/bronze
Leaf color: Green, blue-green
Height: 6 to 12 inches
Plant spacing: 1 to 1½ feet
Notes: Resistant to drought and heat. Do not over-water.

mod. Salt tolerance

Common name: Geranium
Botanical name: *Pelargonium x hortorum*
North Florida planting months: March - April
Central Florida planting months: October - February
South Florida planting months: November - February
Cold tolerance: Tender
Light requirement: Full sun to partial shade
Soil requirements: Well-drained
Flower color: Red, pink, white, salmon, orange, violet, bicolors
Leaf color: Green
Height: 1 to 2 feet
Plant spacing: 1½ to 2 feet
Notes: Tender perennial grown as an annual in north Florida. Remove faded flowers to encourage continual bloom.

**Common name: Gerbera Daisy,
Transvaal Daisy**
Botanical name: *Gerbera jamesonii*
North Florida planting months: March -
   August
Central Florida planting months: February - June
South Florida planting months: November - May
Cold tolerance: Tender
Light requirement: Full sun to partial shade
Soil requirements: Well-drained
Flower color: White, red, orange, yellow,
   salmon, pink
Leaf color: Green
Height: 6 inches
Plant spacing: 12 to 18 inches
Notes: Very lightly damaged by root-knot
   nematodes. Set plants in the ground so that
   the crown is slightly above or level with the
   soil.

**Common name: German Violet,
Persian Violet**
Botanical name: *Exacum affine*
North Florida planting months: April - May,
   August - September
Central Florida planting months: March -
   April, September - October
South Florida planting months: October -
   January
Cold tolerance: Tender
Light requirement: Partial shade
Soil requirements: Well-drained
Flower color: White, lavender, blue, purple
Leaf color: Green
Height: 6 inches to 2 feet
Plant spacing: 6 to 12 inches
Notes: Best used as a houseplant.

Common name: Globe Amaranth
Botanical name: *Gomphrena globosa*
North Florida planting months: April - Septem-
   ber
Central Florida planting months: February -
   March, September - October
South Florida planting months: Year-round
Cold tolerance: Tender
Light requirement: Full sun
Soil requirements: Well-drained
Flower color: Purple, white, pink, lavender,
   red, orange
Leaf color: Green
Height: 1 to 2 feet
Plant spacing: 1 to 1½ feet
Notes: Very lightly damaged by root-knot nema-
   todes. Tolerates poor soils, heat and drought.

Common name: Godetia, Satin Flower
Botanical name: *Clarkia amoena*
North Florida planting months: April - June
Central Florida planting months: February -
  March, November - December
South Florida planting months: November -
  March
Cold tolerance: Hardy
Light requirement: Full sun
Soil requirements: Well-drained
Flower color: Pink, red, white, purple, bicolors
Leaf color: Green
Height: 6 inches to 2 feet
Plant spacing: 6 to 12 inches
Notes: Lightly damaged by root-knot nema-
  todes. Flowers best when temperatures are
  cool.

• •

Common name: Goldenrod
Botanical name: *Solidago* spp.
North Florida planting months: April - July
Central Florida planting months: March - July
South Florida planting months: February - July
Cold tolerance: Tender
Light requirement: Full sun to partial shade
Soil requirements: Well-drained
Flower color: Yellow, orange-yellow, orange
Leaf color: Green
Height: 1 to 6 feet
Plant spacing: 1 to 2 feet
Notes: Often mistakenly believed to cause hay
  fever. Self-sows prolifically and may be
  invasive. Flowers in the fall.

• •

Common name: Heliotrope
Botanical name: *Heliotropium arborescens*
North Florida planting months: March - May
Central Florida planting months: March -
  May, September - October
South Florida planting months: February -
  March
Cold tolerance: Tender
Light requirement: Full sun
Soil requirements: Fertile, moist, well-drained
Flower color: White, dark blue, purple
Leaf color: Glossy, dark green
Height: 1 to 2 feet
Plant spacing: 1 foot
Notes: Produces clusters of tiny, fragrant flowers.

Common name: Hollyhock
Botanical name: *Alcea rosea*
North Florida planting months: April - May
Central Florida planting months: Not recommended
South Florida planting months: Not recommended
Cold tolerance: Hardy
Light requirement: Full sun to partial shade
Soil requirements: Well-drained
Flower color: Red, yellow, white, pink, salmon, purple, lavender, orange
Leaf color: Green
Height: 2 to 9 feet
Plant spacing: 6 to 12 inches
Notes: Heavily damaged by root-knot nematodes. Flowers can be single, semi-double, or fully double.

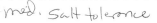

med. salt tolerance

Common name: Impatiens
Botanical name: *Impatiens wallerana*
North Florida planting months: April - August
Central Florida planting months: March - April, September - November
South Florida planting months: September - February
Cold tolerance: Tender
Light requirement: Partial shade to full shade
Soil requirements: Well-drained, moist soil
Flower color: Red, white, pink, salmon, purple, lavender, orange
Leaf color: Green
Height: 6 inches to 2 feet
Plant spacing: 12 to 18 inches
Notes: Best flowering annual for shade. Requires plenty of moisture, especially during the heat of summer. Planted in full sun in south Florida in winter.

mod. salt tolerant

Common name: Kalanchoe
Botanical name: *Kalanchoe blossfeldiana*
North Florida planting months: May - July
Central Florida planting months: May - September
South Florida planting months: September - April
Cold tolerance: Tender
Light requirement: Full sun to partial shade
Soil requirements: Well-drained
Flower color: Orange, pink, red, yellow, salmon
Leaf color: Green, gray-green
Height: 6 to 12 inches
Plant spacing: 6 to 12 inches
Notes: Excellent plant for containers.

Common name: Kale (Ornamental), Ornamental Cabbage
Botanical name: *Brassica oleracea*
North Florida planting months: October - December
Central Florida planting months: November - February
South Florida planting months: November - February
Cold tolerance: Hardy
Light requirement: Full sun
Soil requirements: Well-drained
Flower color: Yellow
Leaf color: Blue-green, green, purple/red, variegated
Height: 6 to 12 inches
Plant spacing: 12 to 18 inches
Notes: Can bolt in hot weather, producing tiny flowers instead of colorful foliage. Color compromised if overnight lows are +55°F.

Salt tolerant - high

Common name: Lisianthus
Botanical name: *Eustoma grandiflorum* (*Lisianthus russellianus*)
North Florida planting months: April - July
Central Florida planting months: March - May
South Florida planting months: February - April, October - November
Cold tolerance: Tender
Light requirement: Full sun to partial shade
Soil requirements: Well-drained, high pH
Flower color: Purple, white, pink, lavender, bicolors
Leaf color: Blue-green, green
Height: 1 to 2 feet
Plant spacing: 6 to 12 inches
Notes: Excellent cut flowers.

Common name: Lobelia
Botanical name: *Lobelia erinus*
North Florida planting months: March - April
Central Florida planting months: February - March, September - October
South Florida planting months: October - February
Cold tolerance: Tender
Light requirement: Full sun to partial shade
Soil requirements: Well-drained, occasionally wet
Flower color: Red, white, blue, pink, purple, lilac
Leaf color: Green
Height: 12 inches
Plant spacing: 6 to 12 inches
Notes: Very heavily damaged by root-knot nematodes. Does not withstand heat well.

Common name: Marigold
Botanical name: *Tagetes* spp.
North Florida planting months: May - June
Central Florida planting months: April - June
South Florida planting months: October - March
Cold tolerance: Tender
Light requirement: Full sun
Soil requirements: Well-drained, tolerates dry soils
Flower color: Yellow, orange
Leaf color: Green
Height: 1 to 3 feet
Plant spacing: 1 to 1½ feet
Notes: Not damaged by root-knot nematodes. Summer heat can cause a temporary decline in flowering. Susceptible to spider mites.

Common name: Mealycup Sage, Blue Salvia, Blue Sage
Botanical name: *Salvia farinacea*
North Florida planting months: March - August
Central Florida planting months: September - March
South Florida planting months: January - March, October - November
Cold tolerance: Tender
Light requirement: Full sun
Soil requirements: Well-drained
Flower color: Blue, white
Leaf color: Green
Height: 2 to 3 feet
Plant spacing: 6 to 12 inches
Notes: Very lightly damaged by root-knot nematodes. Flowers are good for cutting.

Common name: Melampodium, Bush Zinnia
Botanical name: *Melampodium paludosum*
North Florida planting months: April - July
Central Florida planting months: March - July
South Florida planting months: March - August
Cold tolerance: Tender
Light requirement: Full sun
Soil requirements: Well-drained
Flower color: Yellow
Leaf color: Light green
Height: Up to 3 feet
Plant spacing: 12 to 18 inches
Notes: Tolerates heat, drought and poor soil. Self sows and can become weedy.

Common name: Mexican Sunflower
Botanical name: *Tithonia rotundifolia*
North Florida planting months: May - July
Central Florida planting months: April - July
South Florida planting months: March - August
Cold tolerance: Tender
Light requirement: Full sun
Soil requirements: Well-drained, fertile, and dry
Flower color: Deep orange with yellow-orange centers
Leaf color: Dark green
Height: 4 to 6 feet
Plant spacing: 2 feet
Notes: Resistant to heat and drought. Faintly fragrant flowers attract butterflies. Life of cut flowers can be lengthened by searing hollow stems.

• •

Common name: Nasturtium
Botanical name: *Tropaeolum majus*
North Florida planting months: October - February
Central Florida planting months: October - February
South Florida planting months: November - February
Cold tolerance: Hardy
Light requirement: Full sun
Soil requirements: Moist and well-drained
Flower color: Pink, white, red, orange, yellow, mahogany, some bicolored
Leaf color: Dark green
Height: 12 to 15 inches
Plant spacing: 1 foot
Notes: Heavily damaged by root-knot nematodes. Tolerates poor, sandy soils. Flowering ceases when subjected to prolonged heat.

• •

Common name: New Guinea Impatiens
Botanical name: *Impatiens x New Guinea Hybrids*
North Florida planting months: May - July
Central Florida planting months: March - April, September - November
South Florida planting months: October - April
Cold tolerance: Tender
Light requirement: Partial shade
Soil requirements: Well-drained
Flower color: Pink, white, red, lavender, orange, purple
Leaf color: Green, bicolors or tricolored stripes of red, yellow, bronze or purple
Height: 1 to 2 feet
Plant spacing: 1 to 1½ feet
Notes: Protect from hot full-afternoon sun.

Common name: Nicotiana, Flowering Tobacco, Ornamental Tobacco
Botanical name: *Nicotiana alata*
North Florida planting months: April - Mayt
Central Florida planting months: March - May, September - October
South Florida planting months: February - April, October - November
Cold tolerance: Tender
Light requirement: Partial shade
Soil requirements: Well-drained
Flower color: Red, white, green, pink, salmon
Leaf color: Green
Height: 1 to 3 feet
Plant spacing: 1 to 1½ feet
Notes: Moderately damaged by root-knot nematodes. Pleasant fragrance especially noticeable in the evening.

Common name: Ornamental Pepper, Bush Red Pepper
Botanical name: *Capsicum annuum*
North Florida planting months: April - June
Central Florida planting months: February - May, September - October
South Florida planting months: October - May
Cold tolerance: Tender
Light requirement: Full sun
Soil requirements: Well-drained
Flower color: White, green, yellow, orange, red, purple, black fruits.
Leaf color: Green
Height: 1 to 1½ feet
Plant spacing: 6 to 12 inches
Notes: One of the most heat-tolerant bedding plants.

Common name: Pansy
Botanical name: *Viola x wittrockiana*
North Florida planting months: October - February
Central Florida planting months: November - February
South Florida planting months: November - December
Cold tolerance: Hardy
Light requirement: Full sun to partial shade
Soil requirements: Well-drained
Flower color: Red, yellow, white, blue, pink, purple, orange, lavender, rust/bronze, black, some in combinations
Leaf color: Green
Height: 6 to 12 inches
Plant spacing: 6 to 12 inches
Notes: Heavily damaged by root-knot nematodes. Highly cold resistant. Does not tolerate heat.

Common name: Pentas
Botanical name: *Pentas lanceolata*
North Florida planting months: April - July
Central Florida planting months: March - August
South Florida planting months: Year-round
Cold tolerance: Tender
Light requirement: Full sun to partial shade
Soil requirements: Well-drained
Flower color: Red, pink, lavender, white, purple
Leaf color: Green
Height: 2 to 3 feet
Plant spacing: 1½ to 2 feet
Notes: Attracts hummingbirds and butterflies. Grows back from the roots in spring in central Florida following a freeze.

• •

Common name: Periwinkle, Vinca, Madagascar Periwinkle
Botanical name: *Catharanthus roseus*
North Florida planting months: April - June
Central Florida planting months: March - September
South Florida planting months: September - May
Cold tolerance: Tender
Light requirement: Full sun
Soil requirements: Well-drained
Flower color: White, pink, purple, lavender
Leaf color: Green
Height: 1 to 2 feet
Plant spacing: 1 to 1½ feet
Notes: Very lightly damaged by root-knot nematodes. Resistant to heat, drought, insects and pollution.

• •

Common name: Petunia
Botanical name: *Petunia x hybrida*
North Florida planting months: October - February
Central Florida planting months: October - March
South Florida planting months: November - February
Cold tolerance: Hardy
Light requirement: Full sun to partial shade
Soil requirements: Well-drained
Flower color: Red, yellow, white, pink, salmon, purple, lavender; solid and bicolors
Leaf color: Green
Height: ½ to 1½ feet
Plant spacing: 6 to 12 inches
Notes: Lightly damaged by root-knot nematodes. Pinch developing plants to encourage bushy growth.

49

Common name: Purslane
Botanical name: *Portulaca oleracea*
North Florida planting months: April - July
Central Florida planting months: April - May, September - October
South Florida planting months: March - May, October - November
Cold tolerance: Tender
Light requirement: Full sun
Soil requirements: Well-drained, sandy, and dry
Flower color: Bright yellow
Leaf color: Green with reddish stems
Height: 6 to 9 inches
Plant spacing: 10 to 12 inches
Notes: Lightly damaged by root-knot nematodes. Very frost-tender.

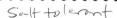

Salt tolerant

Common name: Rose Moss, Moss Rose, Portulaca
Botanical name: *Portulaca grandiflora*
North Florida planting months: April - July
Central Florida planting months: April - May, September - October
South Florida planting months: March - May, October - November
Cold tolerance: Tender
Light requirement: Full sun
Soil requirements: Well-drained
Flower color: Orange, pink, red, yellow, white, salmon, lavender, purple
Leaf color: Green
Height: 6 inches
Plant spacing: 1 to 1½ feet
Notes: Lightly damaged by root-knot nematodes. Makes an excellent ground cover for sunny dry areas.

mod. salt tol.

Common name: Scarlet Sage, Scarlet Salvia, Red Salvia
Botanical name: *Salvia splendens*
North Florida planting months: April - August
Central Florida planting months: February - April, September - October
South Florida planting months: February - November
Cold tolerance: Tender
Light requirement: Full sun to partial shade
Soil requirements: Well-drained
Flower color: Red, white, salmon, purple, pink, lavender
Leaf color: Green
Height: 1 to 3 feet
Plant spacing: 6 to 12 inches
Notes: Very lightly damaged by root-knot nematodes. Attracts hummingbirds. Cut back to produce second and third flower display.

Common name: Shasta Daisy
Botanical name: *Chrysanthemum x superbum*
North Florida planting months: October - December
Central Florida planting months: October - December
South Florida planting months: Not recommended
Cold tolerance: Hardy
Light requirement: Full sun to partial shade
Soil requirements: Well-drained
Flower color: White
Leaf color: Green
Height: 1 to 2 feet
Plant spacing: 2 to 3 feet
Notes: Lightly damaged by root-knot nematodes. Excellent cut flower.

• •

Common name: Silk Flower, Annual Hibiscus
Botanical name: *Abelmoschus moschatus*
North Florida planting months: May - July
Central Florida planting months: April - July
South Florida planting months: March - August
Cold tolerance: Tender
Light requirement: Full sun to partial shade
Soil requirements: Well-drained
Flower color: Red or pink with white centers
Leaf color: Deep green
Height: 12 to 15 inches
Plant spacing: 1 foot
Notes: A relative of okra with single flowers that resemble a tropical hibiscus. Excellent tolerance to heavy rain and heat.

• •

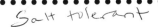
Salt tolerant

Common name: Snapdragon
Botanical name: *Antirrhinum majus*
North Florida planting months: October - March
Central Florida planting months: October - February
South Florida planting months: November - February
Cold tolerance: Hardy
Light requirement: Full sun to partial shade
Soil requirements: Well-drained
Flower color: Red, yellow, white, pink, orange, salmon, lavender, purple
Leaf color: Green
Height: 6 inches to 3 feet
Plant spacing: 6 to 12 inches
Notes: Heavily damaged by root-knot nematodes. Remove spent flowers to improve bloom.

Common name: Spider Flower
Botanical name: *Cleome hasslerana*
North Florida planting months: March - July
Central Florida planting months: March - July
South Florida planting months: March - August
Cold tolerance: Tender
Light requirement: Full sun
Soil requirements: Fertile, well-drained
Flower color: White, rose, pink and lavender
Leaf color: Dark green
Height: 3 to 6 feet
Plant spacing: 1 to 3 feet
Notes: Excellent background plant for beds and borders.

Common name: Statice, Sea-Lavender
Botanical name: *Limonium sinuatum*
North Florida planting months: March - April
Central Florida planting months: December - March
South Florida planting months: September - January
Cold tolerance: Hardy
Light requirement: Full sun
Soil requirements: Well-drained
Flower color: Red, yellow, white, blue, pink, lavender
Leaf color: Green
Height: 1 to 2 feet
Plant spacing: 6 to 12 inches
Notes: Very lightly damaged by root-knot nematodes. Tolerates heat and drought.

Common name: Stock, Gillyflower
Botanical name: *Matthiola incana*
North Florida planting months: April - June
Central Florida planting months: March - May, November - December
South Florida planting months: November - March
Cold tolerance: Hardy
Light requirement: Full sun to partial shade
Soil requirements: Moist, fertile, well-drained
Flower color: Blue, lavender, pink, red, white, yellow
Leaf color: Green
Height: 1 to 3 feet
Plant spacing: 1 to 1½ feet
Notes: Very lightly damaged by root-knot nematodes. Does not flower well in heat. Flowers are extremely fragrant.

Common name: Strawflower
Botanical name: *Helichrysum bracteatum*
North Florida planting months: April - May
Central Florida planting months: March - April
South Florida planting months: November - February
Cold tolerance: Tender
Light requirement: Full sun
Soil requirements: Well-drained
Flower color: Red, yellow, white, pink, salmon, purple, orange
Leaf color: Green
Height: 1 to 3 feet
Plant spacing: 6 to 12 inches
Notes: Very heavily damaged by root-knot nematodes. Tolerates heat and drought.

mod. salt tol.

Common name: Sunflower
Botanical name: *Helianthus annuus*
North Florida planting months: February - April
Central Florida planting months: January - March
South Florida planting months: November - February
Cold tolerance: Tender
Light requirement: Full sun
Soil requirements: Well-drained
Flower color: Yellow, orange, maroon, bronze
Leaf color: Green
Height: 1 to 10 feet
Plant spacing: 1½ to 2 feet
Notes: Heavily damaged by root-knot nematodes. Tolerates heat and drought. Taller cultivars require staking.

Common name: Sweet Pea
Botanical name: *Lathyrus odoratus*
North Florida planting months: October - February
Central Florida planting months: October - February
South Florida planting months: September - February
Cold tolerance: Hardy
Light requirement: Full sun
Soil requirements: Slightly alkaline, fertile and well-drained
Flower color: Purple, rose, red, white, pink, blue
Leaf color: Light green
Height: Vine - 6+ feet; bush - 8 to 30 inches
Plant spacing: Vine - 6 to 8 inches; bush - 15 inches
Notes: Very heavily damaged by root-knot nematodes. Removing seed pods before seeds form will keep sweet peas in bloom.

Common name: Verbena, Garden
Botanical name: *Verbena x hybrida*
North Florida planting months: April - May
Central Florida planting months: February - March, October - November
South Florida planting months: February - April, October - November
Cold tolerance: Hardy
Light requirement: Full sun
Soil requirements: Well-drained
Flower color: White, pink, purple, lavender
Leaf color: Green
Height: 6 to 12 inches
Plant spacing: 2 to 3 feet
Notes: Lightly damaged by root-knot nematodes. Most varieties susceptible to mildew in damp locations with poor air circulation.

Common name: Wishbone Flower, Torenia
Botanical name: *Torenia fournieri*
North Florida planting months: April - June
Central Florida planting months: March - June, September - October
South Florida planting months: February - May, September - October
Cold tolerance: Tender
Light requirement: Full sun to full shade
Soil requirements: Fertile, moist, well-drained
Flower color: White, pink, purple, lavender, yellow
Leaf color: Green
Height: 6 to 18 inches
Plant spacing: 1½ to 2 feet
Notes: Very lightly damaged by root-knot nematodes. Popular for growing in shady locations. Grows best with some shade during the hottest part of the year. Seedlings germinate everywhere close to the plant.

Common name: Zinnia
Botanical name: *Zinnia* spp.
North Florida planting months: April - June
Central Florida planting months: March - April, September - October
South Florida planting months: February - March, September - October
Cold tolerance: Tender
Light requirement: Full sun
Soil requirements: Well-drained and fertile
Flower color: Red, yellow, white, pink, salmon, purple, lavender, orange
Leaf color: Green
Height: 1 to 3 feet
Plant spacing: 1½ to 2 feet
Notes: Very lightly damaged by root-knot nematodes. Pinch young plants to encourage denser plant and more blooms. Remove spent flowers.

Planting Designs

Creating an attractive flower garden requires a carefully considered design or plan. Start by deciding the placement of your flower beds. Remember that in small yards, border and corner beds are the most appropriate, while island beds are best suited for large yards.

Once you've selected the areas for planting, draw a sketch of your garden, noting the approximate dimensions and shapes of the beds. Models for border, corner and island beds, using either cool season or warm season bedding plants, are presented on pages 56 - 61. Sample plant combinations for both north and south Florida gardens are also provided, however these are only a few of the assortments that are possible. New varieties of bedding plants come on the market every year, and you may enjoy mixing these with tried-and-true favorites. Private and public gardens are also good sources for ideas on flower combinations you may want to try. While finalizing your design, it is a good idea to visit your local nurseries and garden supply stores to see what colors and kinds of bedding plants they have.

Border Landscape Design

Warm Season
North Florida Gardens
1. White Spider Flower
2. Yellow Tall Marigolds
3. White Nicotiana
4. Orange Zinnia
5. Orange Cockscomb Celosia
6. Red Salvia
7. Pink Periwinkle
8. Dusty Miller

Warm Season
South Florida Gardens
1. Mexican Sunflower
2. Salvia
3. Coleus
4. Salvia
5. Orange Cockscomb Celosia
6. Torenia
7. Pink Periwinkle
8. Zinnia

In a **border design**, plants are displayed against a backdrop. The backdrop could be a wall, a fence or a border of shrubs. Leaving a space between the back of the bed and the backdrop will allow easy access for weeding, mulching, watering, etc. Remember to stagger plants, keeping shorter ones in the front and the taller ones toward the back of the bed.

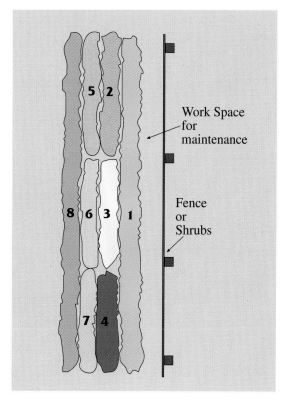

Work Space for maintenance

Fence or Shrubs

Cool Season
North Florida Gardens
1. Orange Tall Snapdragon
2. Yellow Calendula
3. Red Dianthus
4. Yellow Calendula
5. Red Petunia
6. Yellow Pansy
7. Red Petunia
8. White Alyssum

Cool Season
South Florida Gardens
1. Red Nicotiana
2. Yellow Nasturtium
3. Blue Daze
4. Yellow Nasturtium
5. Purple Petunia
6. Red Dianthus
7. Purple Petunia
8. White Alyssum

Corner Landscape Design

Warm Season
North Florida Gardens
1. Tall Pink Zinnia
2. Red Salvia
3. Yellow Plume Celosia
4. White Begonia
5. Pink Begonia

Warm Season
South Florida Gardens
1. Red Pentas
2. Blue Salvia
3. White Periwinkle
4. Red Salvia
5. Lavender Periwinkle

A **corner bed** is triangular in shape and usually has curved front sides. As with border beds, the plants should be arranged with the shortest in the front and the taller ones in the back of the bed. Corner beds are especially attractive if they are terraced. Using garden timbers, stones or railroad ties to form the terraces, you can create a bed where low-growing plants can be used at different levels.

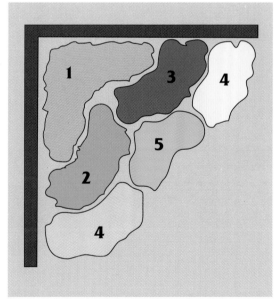

Cool Season
North Florida Gardens
1. Pink Tall Snapdragon
2. Purple Petunia
3. Pink Petunia
4. Yellow Pansy
5. White Candytuft

Cool Season
South Florida Gardens
1. Blue Salvia
2. Pink Impatiens
3. Zinnia
4. Cream Gazania
5. Verbena 'Imagination'

Island Landscape Design

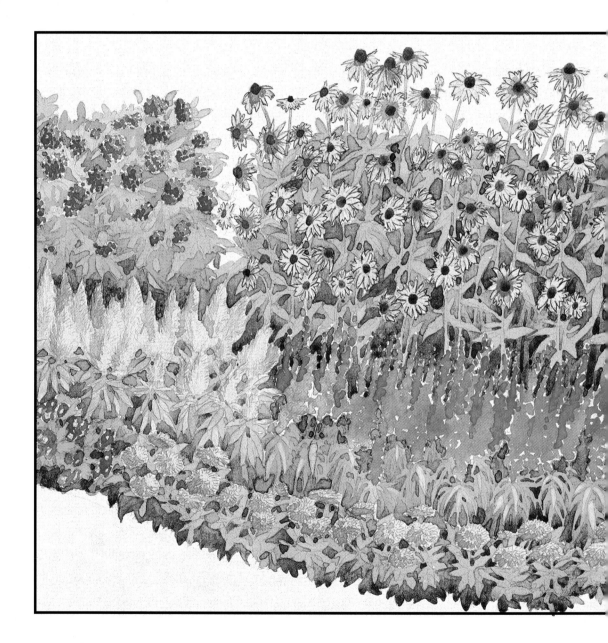

Warm Season
North Florida Gardens

1. Yellow Dwarf Zinnia
2. Red Begonia
3. Yellow Dwarf Plume Celosia
4. Black-Eyed Susan
5. Red Pentas
6. Red Salvia

Warm Season
South Florida Gardens

1. Red Gazania
2. Yellow Purslane
3. Coleus (Red & Yellow Variegation)
4. Mexican Sunflower
5. Red Pentas
6. Blue Daze

An **island bed** can be round, square, rectangular or kidney-shaped. Because island beds are viewed from all directions, tall plants should be placed in the center, medium height plants on all sides and dwarf plants at the edges of the bed. Island beds are easy to maintain because the plants are accessible from all sides.

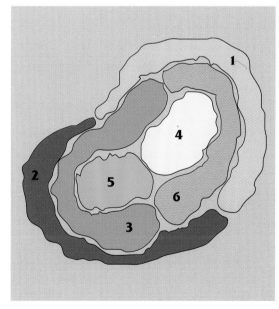

Cool Season

North Florida Gardens

1. Pink Alyssum
2. White Candytuft
3. Blue Pansy
4. Shasta Daisy
5. Orange Snapdragon
6. Purple Petunia

Cool Season

South Florida Gardens

1. Red Petunia
2. White Petunia
3. Red Geranium
4. Tall Yellow Marigold
5. Red Nicotaina
6. White Geranium

Planting and Care

Bedding plants purchased in compartmentalized plastic flats may have pot-bound root systems (**Photo 20**). If planted intact, the root system will be slow to establish in the surrounding soil and plants will suffer moisture stress. A preferred method is to loosen and untangle the root system without breaking the soil ball. Plants will usually recover rapidly and become established quickly. Tall and spindly plants should be pruned to half their original size to produce more attractive plants with more flowers (**Photo 22**). Spacing of plants in a bed should be based on the mature size of a particular plant (**Bedding Plant Selection Guide**).

Bedding plants should be watered immediately after planting and daily until they have become established.

After establishment, they should be watered on an "as needed" basis. Wilting will reduce flowering on many bedding plants and should not be allowed to happen. The frequency of irrigation will depend on soil type, exposure to sunlight, kind of bedding plant and season of the year. Some bedding plants growing in full sun during the summer may require daily watering.

Water applied by an overhead sprinkler system can destroy the beauty of a flower bed by causing the flowers to rot or deteriorate rapidly. Bedding plants vary in their sensitivity to damage by overhead irrigation. Geraniums, celosias, marigolds, gerberas, verbenas, petunias, phlox, portulacas, cannas, snapdragons, strawflowers and pentas (**Photo 23**) are very sensitive to damage by overhead irrigation, while begonias, pansies, coleus, impatiens and New Guinea impatiens (**Photo 24**) are tolerant of

Photo 20: Plants purchased in compartmentalized plastic flats may have pot-bound root-systems.

Photo 21: Weeds can be controlled either by mulching, applying preemergence herbicides, and/ or hand weeding.

damage by overhead irrigation. Bedding plants should be watered by hand using a hose with a breaker attached (**Photo 25**) or with a microirrigation system where only the root systems of the plants are wetted and flowers are not disturbed by splashing water from the irrigation system.

Weeds can be controlled either by mulching (**Photo 21**), applying preemergence herbicides and/or hand weeding. Mulches suppress weeds when the mulch material itself is weed-free and applied deeply enough to prevent weed germination or to smother existing smaller weeds. The amount of mulch to apply will depend on the texture and density of the mulch. Compost and many wood and bark mulches are composed of fine particles and should not be applied any

deeper than 2-3 inches (after settling). Excessive amounts of these fine-textured mulches around shallow-rooted plants can suffocate their roots causing chlorosis and poor growth. Mulches composed solely of shredded leaves or small leaves (oak leaves) should never exceed a 2-inch depth. These materials have flat surfaces, and tend to mat together restricting water and air to plant roots. Mulching materials should not come in contact with plant stems. The high moisture environment created by mulch increases the chances of stem rot, which can result in plant death.

Preemergence herbicides can be very effective in managing weeds in bedding plants. In most cases, they should be applied after transplanting bedding plants to weed-free beds.

Photo 22: Tall and spindly plants should be pruned to half their size to produce a more attractive plant with more flowers.

Photo 23: Plants such as these geraniums are sensitive to damage by overhead sprinklers.

Preemergence herbicides act by inhibiting the normal root development of small weeds before they emerge from the soil. In some cases, bedding plant species are tolerant of the herbicide, but more often the plant remains unharmed when herbicide is appropriately applied. Because most weed seeds germinate within the upper half inch of soil, surface herbicide applications control them without injury to the bedding plant, which has roots normally growing well below the treated zone.

A weed management program for bedding plants based on the use of preemergence herbicides is complicated by the diversity of plants usually growing in the same bed. The herbicide may be safe to use on one species in a bed, but can cause severe damage to other species in the same bed. The matter can become even more compli-cated because cultivars of the same species can respond quite differently to the same herbicide. In order to reduce the chances of damage, always check the label of an herbicide to see if it is registered for use on the plant species growing in a bed. If a species does not appear on the herbicide label, it is **illegal** to use the herbicide on that species even though the applicator assumes all risks and liabilities.

Hand weeding can be a very effective component of a weed management program. It should be considered when managing weeds in a few small beds or when herbicides cannot be used. Hand weeding is also a good option when herbicides are not effective in controlling all the weeds in a bed. Cultivation by hoeing and tilling is also effective in controlling small annual weeds. However, cultivation can stimulate the germination of weed seeds and re-

Photo 24: Plants such as these impatiens are very tolerant of damage by overhead sprinklers.

bedding plants in Florida is to grow them in pots. In areas where the soil is very poor or where tree roots limit growth, it is easier to plant small plants into inexpensive plastic pots filled with good soil and place the pots into flower beds (**Photo 26**). Sink pots into the soil until the top surface of the pot is at soil level. In addition to growing bedding plants where normally they will not grow, growing annuals in pots eliminates nematode problems and allows for easy replacement of plants in the flower bed. ■

Photo 25: Bedding plants should be watered by hand using a hose with a breaker attached.

duce the effectiveness of herbicides by disrupting the contact of the herbicide with germinating weed seedlings.

Another approach to the culture of

Photo 26: Where soil is poor or tree roots are present, plants can be placed into the ground in small pots filled with good soil.

Pests and Diseases

Bedding plants may have insect and disease problems. To maintain healthy and attractive plants, these problems must be recognized and control measures initiated.

The best method of reducing insect and/or disease problems is to keep the plants growing vigorously and free from stress. Cultural maintenance practices that should help to reduce insect and disease problems are as follows:

(1) Plant cool-season bedding plants in the fall, winter and early spring and warm-season bedding plants in the spring and summer months;

(2) Select a planting site which provides desirable growing conditions for a particular bedding plant;

(3) Avoid planting in corners where light intensity and air circulation are minimal;

(4) Keep plants growing vigorously by following a regular fertilization and irrigation schedule;

(5) Avoid wilting by regularly watering bedding plants. Plants without adequate water are more susceptible to infestation by thrips and red spider mites;

(6) Remove spent flowers that do not naturally fall from plants such as marigold, salvia, snapdragon and geranium;

(7) Prevent pathogenic fungal spores from germinating by keeping water off plants as much as possible and providing good air circulation around plants by allowing ample space between plants at planting; and

(8) Remove weeds from flower beds since they frequently host insects and/or disease organisms.

Bedding plants should be monitored frequently for insects and diseases. Infestations detected in the early stages can be controlled by spot treatment before the entire flower bed is infested. An insect infestation on a few plants can be controlled by picking insects off by hand or, in the case of disease, by removing infected leaves or plants. For severe infestations, chemical control will be needed. Contact your local County Extension Office for recommendations on selection and application of pesticides.

Literature Cited

1. Dunn, R. A. 1992. Nematode management in landscape ornamentals. RF-NG013. Florida Cooperative Extension Service, University of Florida, Institute of Food and Agricultural Sciences.

2. Tjia, B. and S. A. Rose. 1987. Salt tolerant bedding plants. Proc. Fl. State Hort. Soc. 100: 181-182.

3. Goff, C.C. 1936. Relative susceptability of some annual ornamentals to root knot. University of Florida Agriculture Experimental Station. Bull. 291.

Other Gardening Resources

Publications
Checklist of the Woody Cultivated Plants (SP 33)
Insects and Related Pests of Turfgrass in Florida (SP 140)
Florida Guide to Environmental Landscapes (SP 114)
Florida Lawn Handbook (SP 45)
Your Florida Landscape: A Complete Guide to Planting and Maintenance (SP 135)
Weeds in Florida (SP 37)
Weeds of Southern Turfgrasses (SP 79)

Identification Card Decks
Insect Identification Flash Cards (SP 130)
TroubleShooting Diseases of Flowering Plants (SP 162)
Troubleshooting Lawn Pests (SP 180)

Computer Software
E-Scape: Environmental Landscaping Computer Game (SW 90)
Fairs CD-ROM Multimedia Database (SW 77)
Plant It: An Interactive Multimedia CD-ROM Plant Selector (SW 85)
Plantsel: Landscape Plant Selector (SW 79)

To order copies of the above items, or for information on other books, manuals, videos, CD-ROMS, flash cards and other media related to agriculture and natural resources, send $1 to:

Resources Catalogue
Publication Distribution Center, University of Florida
P.O. Box 11011
Gainesville, FL 32611-0011

1-800-226-1764

Index

Index (continued)

Index (continued)

Contributors

Editors
Robin Sweat
Kathryn Schreyer

Graphic Design
David Dishman

Technical Advisor
Teresa Howe

Photographers
Robert Black
Edward Gilman
Teresa Howe
Donna Mitchell

Consultants
Andreas Daehnick
Diane Weigle

Proofreaders
Meredith Bell
Donna Mitchell

Indexers
Mark Tobias
Robin Sweat